Senior

Adult

Ministries

Taking Your Senior Adult
Ministries To the Next Level

Leadership Handbook

Senior Adult Ministries
Leadership Manual

TABLE OF CONTENTS

SAM
Senior Adult Ministries

Preface

First, we need to understand what is happening with our seniors.

Since society has decided anyone 55 (or 50) and older is a senior adult, we are looking at a 40 year (+/-) period. Such a time span allows for multiple generations of the same family to be classified as senior adults. There are currently three generations of senior adults, and a fourth is on the horizon. The G. I. Generation (Government Issue) includes folks born before 1925. The Silent Generation consists of those born between 1926 and 1945. Members of the Baby Boomer Generation were born between 1946 and 1964... 76,000,000 of them. Each generation has its own unique values and interests, developed because of historical events or societal trends of their formative years. These values and interests will, in turn, influence what seniors will like to do. The church today should learn all we can about these generations.

The generation to watch closely is Baby Boomers: Born 1946 to 1964. The first of the Baby Boomers began turning 65 years of age on January 1, 2011. Every day in the United States 10,000 people are celebrating their 65th birthday. On May 10, 2017 the U.S. population was estimated to be 325,019,850. Of that total population, 54,872,341 are 65 and older (nearly 17% of the U.S. population). However, by the year 2020 that number is expected to be over 74,000,000, with the U.S. population being approximately 335,765,000 (over 22% will be over 65, nearly one in four persons). Almost one quarter of the average American's life will be spent in retirement.

Statistics from the United States Department of Health and Human Services show that from 1900 to 2004 life expectancy increased from 47.6 to 78.4 years of age.

The economy and lower fertility rates in the U.S. have led to a decline in the birth rate. The result is an increase in the senior adults, and decrease in the children and youth in the United States. For the first time in the history of our nation, there are more senior citizens than teenagers. In addition, accordingly, we now have an urgent need for more consideration to be given to the fastest growing population, which is the Senior Adults.

In our churches today, we have wonderful nursery, children's, youth, and young adult ministries. And, while we have men's and women's ministries, they are not specifically tailored to senior adults. Accordingly, some of our seniors do not attend these ministries.

It is true that many of our churches have some form of seniors' ministry; however, those ministries are typically limited to a once-a-month breakfast, or lunch, and very little more.

As our churches have intentionally sought for ways to reach the Millennials, Gen X and Gen Y age groups, some have unintentionally driven away many of the senior adults in our churches.

Research shows these Boomers are very different from past seniors. They are better educated, healthier, living longer, more active, more financially secure and have much more to offer than previous generations, and they want to use their talents, abilities, and spiritual gifts.

The desire of the Senior Adult Ministries Department of the Assemblies of God is to offer a model for our churches to build upon in the establishment of their own Seniors' Ministry for their church.

In King David's prayer for himself, and against the enemies of his soul, he wrote the following:

"Do not cast me away when I am old; do not forsake me when my strength is gone."
Psalm 71:9

Who

There appears to be quite a variation on what the age of a "senior adult" should be in our society.

The American Association of Retired Persons (AARP) is open for enrollment of persons age 50 and over. Some establishments will honor and give discounts to those who are 55, while others consider 60 more appropriate. Since the Social Security Administration considered 65 to be retirement age for many years, that has also been the age many consider more appropriate.

However, unlike many of the ministries within our Fellowship for boys and girls clubs, Sunday school and Christian education classes, nursery, children's, youth, Fine Arts, and so forth, Senior Adult Ministries can begin at any reasonable age you choose.

You may have several hundred seniors in your church, and might consider separating them into age groups closer to their peers. Or, you may want to keep them all together to increase the numbers involved in the various ministries your group will have.

As you can see, there is no fixed rule to follow. Just do what is best for your church, and your group.

What

The "What" will depend on the desires of the group. The Seniors' Ministries belongs to "them". "They" need to take ownership in it, for it to be most effective.

Below are a few suggestions of ministries your group may want to be involved in:

1. Bring seniors into greater participation with the total church life

2. Discipleship opportunities (within and outside the church)

3. Senior parking lot greeters

4. Senior ushers

5. Form a Seniors Choir

6. Form a Seniors Orchestra

7. Disaster relief volunteers, and RVers

8. Ministry to widows and orphans

9. Study health issues

10. Study foods that heal

11. Transportation for older seniors

12. Free, Wills and Living Wills

13. Grief classes

14. Community projects

15. Help each other with their "To Do" lists

16. Day trips

17. Missionary liaisons (for supported missionaries)

18. Mission's trips

19. Holy Land tours

20. Clean Assisted Living/Nursing Homes

21. Bring fruit/flowers/candy to shut-ins (as appropriate)

22. "On-call" helper, guys (tripped breaker, flat tire…)

23. "On-call" helper gals (light housecleaning, cooking…)

24. Bible study/book study

25. Soup kitchen volunteers

26. Daily light exercise classes

27. Church-school teacher's helper/substitute

28. Phone calls and cards

29. Hospital & Nursing Home visits

30. Church maintenance and landscaping

31. Prison ministry

32. Nursery Attendants

33. Kid's Camp Grandparents

34. Church office assistance (folding bulletins, etc.)

35. Prayer teams and altar workers

36. Hospitality ministry

37. Newly married/young adult marriage conference leaders

38. ???

As you can see, the list can go on and on. Have as many as possible, as often as possible, to include as many seniors (and their friends) as you can.

Don't try to lead everything yourself. Personally ask someone involved in each ministry to lead that ministry. Also, don't forget to train those ministry leaders; and don't forget to honor and thank those ministry leaders… often!

When

Every day. Every week. Some will only be available on different days of the week, and at different times of the day. Don't dictate the time and place, let the seniors choose what works best for them.

Most of your seniors may be retired, but don't forget they still have a life and other obligations to attend to.

The objective of a Senior Adult Ministry is to bless the folks involved in it, as they bless others they are serving. That can happen seven days a week, and twenty-four hours a day for some of them.

Can't sleep? Get up and write a note to a missionary family. Pray for that friend who was just admitted to the hospital. Pray for the pastor and staff. You can do many 3:00 a.m. things.

Where

At the church. In the community. On the Via Dolorosa. In El Salvador or Honduras.

Anywhere. Everywhere. Be creative. Be adventurous.

Why

Because fellowship is a lost commodity in this digital age in which we live, and, because our Lord and Savior, Jesus Christ, desires for us to take the gospel outside the four walls of the church.

Also, Senior Adult Ministries is an excellent evangelistic outreach to bring our friends, relatives, former (and current) business associates, and neighbors to the saving knowledge of our Lord and Savior.

Because it gives others the opportunity to see Christ in action through us.

Because it offers us the opportunity to help others, who may have to do without, due to their inability to accomplish the task(s) themselves.

Because, "by this may all men will know that we are His disciples".

Because there are still unreached people (seniors) living around our churches.

Because, as Superintendent Ken Burtram said at the *Beyond 100* Celebration of the Potomac Ministry Network, "Each generation must shoulder the spiritual responsibility for the church which Jesus bought with His own precious blood."

How

By raising up servant leaders to fulfill their dreams of being involved in a worthwhile ministry that is bigger than themselves.

By working together for the upbuilding of the kingdom of God.

By submitting ourselves to the purpose for which God created us.

Thoughts Regarding a Senior Adult Ministry

One ministry with great potential within our society is ministry to senior adults.

Statistics help to put this potential in perspective:

• 34% of all Americans are 50 years of age or older (that's over 1 in 3 people).

• Every 7 seconds another person turns 50! *(12,342.86 per day)*

• People age - 65 plus - number over 54 million representing nearly one out of every 5 Americans.

• The number of older Americans (65+) has increased to 12.4% since 1990 (3.3 million). This number is expected to grow to 27% by 2030

• In the U.S., 3.6 million people celebrated their 65th birthday last year …10,000 per day. The last of the Baby Boomers will not reach age 65 until 2029.

• As of July 1983, there were more adults age 65 or older, than teenagers in the United States.

• This growing number of senior adults is living longer than ever before. More than two hundred Americans reach age 100 each week.

Senior Adult Ministries
Leadership Manual

Do not rebuke an older man, but exhort him as a father and older women as mothers with all purity. 1 Timothy 5:1

Senior citizens (defined here as those over 65) are the fastest growing age segment of American society. The so-called "age wave" which is breaking over our society means that one in three Americans is over 50, and one in five is over 65.

There are more Americans over 65 than total residents of Canada today!

If we as the church are to reach our society, this means that we should have a well-thought-out strategy for ministering to seniors, and by seniors. Less than one third of Assemblies of God churches have some form of Senior Adult Ministries currently, and most of those have very limited activities.

What do we need to know about senior ministry?

- Seniors have many spiritual needs. In our youth-oriented society, they often feel ignored, left out and rejected. Loneliness is an increasing problem of seniors as they age.

- Seniors are only one step away from eternity. We must reach them with the Gospel before they stand before Christ.

- Seniors possess the most valuable commodity of our day in abundance... time. They have time to serve, time to share, and time to minister. While others today are constantly time-starved, many seniors sit around with time on their hands, and nothing to do. What a resource awaiting the church, time to be tapped, or time to be wasted!

- Seniors have a special opportunity to be prayer warriors, and to devote themselves to the things of God. Paul envisioned a ministry of senior women "who devote themselves to prayer night and day" (1 Timothy 5:5).

- Many seniors have an abundance of experience with the things of God. They have lived and walked with the Lord for decades. Their wisdom needs to be passed down through a growing church, to help develop others.

One or more of the five values that form the foundation of most of their meaningful activities motivate older adults:

- Autonomy---they desire to be or remain self-sufficient.

- Social and spiritual connectedness---they respond to people more than programs.

- Altruism---they desire to give something back to the world.

- Personal growth---they desire to continue developing as human beings.

- Revitalization---they respond to activities that bring fresh and new experiences.

Effective older adult ministries in the twenty-first century will be those that integrate these values and motivators into a creative variety of activities and experiences.

OTHER THOUGHTS ABOUT A SENIOR ADULT MINISTRY IN YOUR CHURCH!

The greatest opportunity for the church to reap a harvest in the next 20 years will be in the area of reaching the senior adult population! Why? Because they are the fastest growing segment of the population. Over 70,000 people are over 100 years of age. There are more people over 65 years of age than under 18. Additionally, at least 10,000 people turn 50 and 65 every day in America. The senior adult population is growing three times faster than all of the other age groups! The senior adult is often the forgotten part of the church. Relegated to the back pews, many seniors are not involved in church planning or programs. Yet, approximately 70% of the average church budget comes from those 55 and older. Seniors have the TIME, TALENTS AND TREASURES to bless the church of today and tomorrow.

We believe that God wants us to be fishers of "all men." The church that neglects the senior adult population will be missing a great opportunity to capture the wisdom of this group. The world recognizes the advantage of reaching this age group. Marketing is geared more and more toward senior adults. They recognize the experience and work ethic of many senior adults and want them for employees. Opportunities to reach senior adults are everywhere. Every church in the Assemblies of God Fellowship needs to prayerfully consider beginning a ministry to the senior adults in their church and in their community. God has not given up on the senior adults, will the church? At the General Council level we stand ready to assist the local pastor and congregation to have a vibrant and effective ministry to senior adults. Truly, the fields are white (with age) unto harvest. Please help us pray, plan, and prepare for the harvest.

At the *Beyond 100* celebration in the Potomac Ministry Network our General Superintendent said, "The Holy Spirit is seeing things that we do not see"; and, then he said, "Let's make room for creativity and the people to whom the Spirit is speaking to."

I pray He is speaking to you about starting, or enlarging, your Senior Adult Ministry.

WHAT TO DO FIRST!

Someone once said, "You can do more after you pray, but you cannot do anything UNTIL you pray!" Prayer is the most important thing you can do as you begin a Senior Adult Ministry! Every church and community is different. That is why we need God to lead us into a new ministry. Then we CAN do some things!

We will start with five KEY elements that all successful Senior Adult Ministries have in common. Whether you have 5 or 500 seniors, there are some basic things you need to include in your planning to start a senior adult ministry.

1. INVOLVE CHURCH LEADERSHIP

It is important that the pastor and church leaders see the need to reach out to seniors. The National Headquarters of the Assemblies of God begin their Senior Adult Ministry at 50 years old. Some church groups start at ages 55 or 60. Wherever you want to start is all right - just start. Perhaps there is someone in your congregation that has shown an interest or burden for "older" people. It may be a younger couple who God can use to lead your group. However God leads, the pastor and leaders of the church need to be involved. Talk to the leaders of your church. Most pastors will support and be glad for someone to begin a ministry to senior adults. However, if they are not, it will be difficult to get much support and encouragement. That is why prayer is vitally important to the beginning of a new ministry.

What should you look for in a leader for this new group? There are four qualities that a leader to senior adults should have:

a. A LOVE for seniors. As with any age group, people can sense if a person is doing a ministry out of duty or devotion. Love must be the beginning of a great Senior's Ministry.

b. The Senior adult leader must LIKE being around the seniors. Most seniors enjoy talking about what has happened during their lifetime. They love to sing the old hymns, talk about camp meetings, and going to revivals. Seniors' children and grandchildren often play an important role in their life. The senior leader must enjoy talking and, most importantly, listening to this group.

c. The leader must also be willing to "LET GO" and share responsibility with others in the group. Giving an opportunity for those who have the talents and wisdom in different areas to bless others will be a key factor in developing a strong ministry to seniors. This will have a two-fold effect. Not only will the person have an opportunity to be used of God, but the group will be stronger as a whole by using others' strengths rather than one person trying to do it all.

d. A good leader will also be someone who is willing to LEARN new information. The senior of today has different needs than the seniors of a generation ago. There are lots of new resources and materials available that a person can learn how to reach out to today's seniors.

As was mentioned earlier, age should not be the sole factor in selecting a leader. Someone with a love and desire to reach out to this group is what you want. Some older person who has a vision but not enough physical strength would be good as an advisor, but not the leader. In addition, the leader must also be willing to learn and try new ways of reaching people. Perhaps God already has someone in your congregation who, with the right encouragement and training, could be a great leader to the group and a blessing to the church and community.

2. MEET WITH INTERESTED INDIVIDUALS

Announce a meeting for all those interested in helping form, or getting more information about starting a Senior Adult Ministry. Again, anyone can come, and having people of different ages can give balance and fresh insight into forming a new ministry. This meeting is important and needs to be prepared for with much prayer and planning.

Before this meeting the leader should do some research in several areas. You need to develop a profile of seniors in the local church and community. Here`s some information you should come prepared to share with the group: How many adults are connected with the church who are 50-65 years of age? How many live in the community who are that age? How many adults are connected with the church who are 65+? How many live in the community who are that age? You can usually find demographic information at the public library, chamber of commerce or city hall.

What is the potential for ministry to senior adults in the community? Is the town made up of younger or older people? As you begin to become known as a church that is interested in, and reaching out to, senior adults, some people will come to you and want to be a part of your senior adult ministry. What ministries are senior adults currently being used in at the church? What could they be doing? What are other congregations in your community doing to reach older adults? Talk to other churches and see what is working and what is not!

EVALUATE WHERE YOU ARE IN
MINISERING TO SENIORS!

PRIORITIZE THE NEEDS. START WITH
YOUR CHURCH`S SENIORS!

BRAINSTORM ABOUT NEW MINISTRIES

3. RECRUIT LEADERSHIP FROM WITHIN THE ADULT GROUP

You may already have the makings of a dynamic senior adult group in your church. Retired farmers, businesspersons, secretaries, teachers, homemakers, health care workers, etc. These people have a lifetime of experience and wisdom. It is up to the leader to give them an opportunity for ministry in and outside the church. Don`t necessarily pick someone you think would be a good leader. Pray, and ask God to bring the leaders to you who will want to serve and use their talents. It may surprise you who will come forth to serve. Many seniors, both in the church and in the community, want to "give back" in life what they have learned.

4. DEVELOP A NAME, MISSION, AND VISION STATEMENT

Ask the group to come up with a name for the group and a mission statement (see page 20). What name would represent the purpose for the group starting? Pick a Bible passage to support your group's name and mission. Every group should begin with soul-winning and outreach as a PRIMARY goal of the group. Some groups just become a "bless me club" and become stagnant. God will bless a group that wants to reach out to the lost and hurting. The group should understand that from the very beginning they will want to reach out to everyone they can. What do you want to see God accomplish in and through your group?

5. ORGANIZE SEVERAL GROUPS AROUND MINISTRY GOALS

Most growing senior adult groups have four-six aspects to them. Just as one size shoe does not fit everyone, so you will want to have enough interest groups to appeal to everyone. One suggestion would be to take a survey and see what the seniors in your church are interested in. Some will want to come together to study the Bible. Another group may want to come together for social reasons, trips, activities, etc. Another will be missions and evangelistic in emphasis. Serving in the church through various ways may be one group's interest. Many seniors are interested in learning new things, so providing learning opportunities is a great way to reach seniors outside the church. Each church will be different but you want leaders for each of the groups mentioned. Again, prayer will be crucial for God to send you leaders in the various areas. As you get leaders for the various groups they will begin to take ownership of their group and it can grow! If you only have a few seniors you may want to start with only one or two different groups, but get ready for more seniors to start coming!

The task is a great one! However, most senior groups started small. Don`t worry about the number of people or ministries you have. Just start and God will bless your efforts.

There are obstacles and barriers in most churches that keep a senior ministry from developing. Learning what these are and how to overcome them is important. We encourage you to constantly be thinking of new ideas and resources to make your Senior's Ministry both interesting and exciting for any size church. Please share with others what you have found here that is helpful, and contact the Senior Adult Ministries national office if we can be of additional help! God bless you!

We would ask you to dream and work with us to reach our seniors for Christ!

Remember, as you begin to become known as a church that is interested in, and reaching out to senior adults, some people will come to you and want to be a part of your senior adult ministry.

As a post-script: **Be sure your facilities are senior adult friendly.**

Older seniors need easily accessible, comfortable, well-lit meeting space with good temperature control. These rooms should be close to the church worship center as well as large, accessible restrooms. Ramps, railings and bright lights are assets. Provide close-in, reserved parking places for seniors near their meeting rooms and the church sanctuary. Be sure parking lots and walkways are well lit. During inclement weather, provide assistance for seniors who need help in navigating stairs and slippery walkways.

Here are Suggestions for Getting Started:

Senior Adult Planning Committee

The pastor and official church board can appoint a senior adult ministry planning committee. This committee will most likely consist of key senior adults in the church, but it may include adults of any age with a concern for and desire to minister to senior adults. The pastor should review with each prospective member, the committee's responsibilities, purpose and length of commitment expected by those serving on the committee. It is also important for the pastor to point out that committee members may or may not be the leadership that eventually is elected or appointed to carry out the ministry. Two essential principles should be kept in mind:

• Pastoral involvement is necessary.

• Plan the program **with** the senior adults - not just **for** them.

Determining the Needs of Senior Adults

The planning committee and coordinator should work together to determine the needs of senior adults. This includes needs and interests of senior adults within the congregation, and in the community. This information can be gathered by research, surveys and interviews, brainstorming by the planning committee, and by observation of senior adults. Remember, it is important to find out what the senior adults themselves would like in a senior adult ministry. One survey determined the following needs ranked according to importance:

• Love and appreciation

• Acknowledgement of usefulness and significance

• Acceptance and respect as a viable group by the church body

• Information and education regarding money, finances, wills and trusts

• Health information

• Transportation

• Counseling about spiritual and family issues

• Recreation

Keeping these needs in mind as you plan your ministry will add to the success of the group. Senior adults need someone to love and appreciate them. Families have scattered, friends have died, and incomes are often limited. Concern and fear can become overwhelming, but friends, spiritual help and Christian fellowship can bring renewal to their hearts and minds. Not all seniors will be as actively involved as others, due to personal circumstances. Remember to keep everyone informed of available ministry, regardless of how often they attend.

Develop Familiarity with Services Provided By Community Agencies

There can be great benefit from programs and services provided by government and voluntary organizations and agencies in your community. Your church may want to research how it could support, assist in or utilize these programs. Check with County Social Services Department, Community Services Department, Council on Aging, the United Way, Health Department and other similar resources. Some agencies may be willing to present workshops and education seminars to your church. Contact local hospitals for literature they may have on such community services such as:

• Dial-a-Ride

• Meals on Wheels

• Legal services

• Nutrition programs

• Winterization programs

• Health care visitation

• Recreational and craft classes

Visit Other Senior Adult Ministry Programs

By visiting other programs in your city or nearby communities, you can benefit from their experience. Look at the strengths or weaknesses of their programs. Determine the methodology they use to carry out their goals and objectives. Ask questions:

• How did you get started?

• What are the greatest needs of this age group?

• What programs did you begin with?

• What are the strengths and weaknesses of your programs?

• What do you know now that you wish you had known at the beginning?

Call an Organizational Meeting with the Senior Adults

This meeting could be held following a covered dish dinner at the church. This is the Planning Committee's opportunity to report on the planning they have done, and what the goal and scope of your ministry might be. Discuss these plans and hear from the group. This kind of interaction is essential! Let them feel like they "own" the program. As attractive as programs may appear in other churches or groups, it is not wise to duplicate them unless you are sure your senior adults want them. Ultimately, the type of program and services offered will depend on your most urgent local interests and needs, and how your senior adults respond at the meeting.

If possible, use this meeting to set up the organization and leadership for your senior adult program. However, it may be necessary to meet again for this purpose. Keep the organization as simple as possible. Elect officers such as director, secretary, and treasurer. Consider finances. Will this ministry be subsidized by the church or self-supporting through fund-raising activities? Also establish guidelines and policies for the program. Who is responsible for what? What are the lines of authority and communication? How will officers be elected? Set up your regular meetings. How frequently will the senior adults meet – daily, weekly, biweekly, or monthly? Where will the meetings be held?

Meet With the Pastor

Meet with your pastor for assistance in your planning for senior adult ministry. When you keep him/her informed, he/she will be better able to promote this ministry. Be prepared for your meeting by organizing the ideas you want to share and compiling a list of questions that you would like to ask such as:

• What church-wide events may we use to inform the congregation of achievements of senior adults?

• How can we eliminate the widespread errors and myths about old age?

• How can senior adults be included in planning programs and ministries designed to meet their needs?

• How does the church assist in educating people about the changing needs of the aging? How could we use a Sunday morning service to inform the congregation about aging and the senior adult?

• How does our church view its senior adults?

• How can our church assist senior adults in handling feelings of guilt that result from the realization that they did not do in their earlier years, what they could have done?

• How can our church's ministry help people answer the question: "What does it mean to grow old?"

Other questions:

_____

_____

_____

_____

_____

_____

_____

_____

_____

_____

_____

_____

_____

_____

_____

_____

Maintain Balance

Never allow your ministry's concern to become so narrow that it over emphasizes certain aspects while under emphasizing other equally important aspects of senior adult life. Consider the following five areas of ministry and seek to maintain an appropriate balance between them.

Spiritual Enrichment

Senior years provide great potential growth. Surveys have indicated that, among the general adult population, the older a person gets the more important religion becomes to their life. Senior adults can become the "pillars of the church". Time pressures and life responsibilities have lessened. Life experiences give deeper meaning to Bible teachings. Give senior adults spiritually enriching activities including Bible studies and special worship opportunities. Events should be planned for evangelism and outreach in the community.

Learning Opportunities

Through formal and informal groups senior adults should be actively involved in learning. It is a myth that senior adults are not interested in learning. Sunday School (or Small Groups) should provide meaningful and appropriate education opportunities. In addition, special workshops and seminars can be provided for the senior adults. It is useful to survey your senior adults to see what topics and subjects are particularly meaningful to them. Involve them in discussion groups and let them view interesting and educational films. Provide audio and videotape/DVD resources in the church library.

Socialization

This is the area most of us think of first concerning senior adult ministry. The need for interaction with other people continues throughout life. Is your ministry providing fulfilling and rewarding social activities? Social activities have great personal health benefits also.

Service Opportunities

Many churches have not begun to tap the potential resources in their older members. The church should not encourage the too frequent message of society that says senior adults have outlived their usefulness. Seniors want and need opportunities to serve as well as be served, to minister as well as be ministered to.

Needed Services

Most senior adult's ministries will be weakest in this area. There are many senior adults who feel "invisible" to the congregation. We must not allow them to be "out of sight, out of mind". What are the medical, financial, and legal services needed for your senior adults? Because there are limitations to what the church can offer, strong working relationships between community services and the church are needed. However, we dare not overlook this area or think that "ministry" cannot or should not be concerned with all aspects of senior adult life.

Senior Adult Ministries: Suggested Committees and Definition of Roles

Senior Adult Coordinator Ministry Description:

(add or delete depending on your specific church needs)

• Work closely with the pastor.

• Serve as the chairperson of the senior adult committee.

• Act as the liaison between the planning committee and the church board.

• Act as the liaison between all church ministries serving senior adults.

• Be informed of community agencies serving the senior adults.

• Correlate and coordinate all the activities of the senior adults.

• Report all senior activities to the church leadership.

• Recommend actions to take to enhance the senior adult ministry.

• Set in motion any new activities.

• Represent senior adults in the church and community.

The Purpose of Senior Adult Ministries is threefold:

To Bring People to Christ

• To bring people to Jesus Christ, and to bring Christians to a closer, more intimate relationship with Him.

To Minister

• Minister to the relational needs of the local church congregation.

• To serve as a vehicle for interaction among the people of this congregation.

To Encourage Others to Minister.

To encourage commitment to ministry in God's kingdom. A light should not be kept under a bushel, but used to the continued service and glory of the Lord.

• To maintain the identity of people with regard to their continued value as vital parts of the body of Christ; to recognize their value in terms of wisdom, experience, knowledge, talents, and other God given abilities and gifts.

* Relational needs will be addressed in many ways including prayer and worship activities, meetings, events, trips, programs, and other areas where Senior Adult Ministries can be of assistance.

"Even as the Son of Man came not to be ministered unto, but to minister,   and to give His life a ransom for many." Matthew 20:28

Possible Committees:

(Others may be added depending on the needs and size of the group.)

Program Committee – Plan programs for special banquets and events

Hospitality Committee – Take care of the food service at the various Senior Adult Ministry functions.

Promotions Committee – Publicizes the events of the Senior Adult Ministry group.

Telephone Committee – Contact all senior adults concerning prayer requests, making announcements, or informing of special events.

Transportation Committee – Be sure all the senior adults have transportation to the various senior adult activities. This is a major problem for many elderly people.

Mission & Vision Statement thoughts:

MISSION STATEMENT: *To provide opportunities for spiritual enrichment; provide social, emotional, and physical activities, make available educational information pertinent to senior adults and provide opportunities for ministry; and ensure no one is lost or forgotten.*

VISION STATEMENT: *We seek to be known throughout our community for our devotion to Jesus Christ and our commitment to share His love by providing comprehensive ministries that reach senior adults to enhance their lives, encourages them to spiritually grow in the Lord, challenges them to serve the Lord with all their heart, mind, soul, and strength, and, allows them every opportunity to share their gifts, wisdom and knowledge with others.*

The Core Values of the Senior Adult Ministry can be summed up as follows:

FELLOWSHIP, sharing of abilities with others for the cause of Christ.

ENCOURAGEMENT, reinforcing one another in need.

COMPASSION, support of the needy. We are care givers, not just care receivers.

OUTREACH, carrying out the Great Commission through our Centers of Influence.

First Church

Your City, State

Ministry Title: **Senior Adult Pastor**

Position Reports to: Lead Pastor (or Executive Pastor)

Ministry Overview

Responsible for correlating and coordinating all Senior Adult Ministry events. Liason between the Lead Pastor and the Senior Adult Ministry Planning Committee.

Principle Accountabilities:

- Works closely with the Lead Pastor
- Serves as the chairperson of the Senior Adult Ministries committee
- Acts as the liaison between the planning committee and the church board
- Acts as the liaison between all church ministries serving senior adults
- Be informed of community agencies serving the senior adults

- Correlates and coordinates all the activities of the senior adults
- Reports all senior adult ministry activities to the church leadership
- Recommend actions to take to enhance the Senior Adult Ministries
- Set in motion any new ministry activities
- Represent senior adults in the church and community

Below is a list of other ministry positions you might want to consider for your Senior Adult Ministries. The Ministry Overview and Principle Accountabilities will differ from church to church, depending on several factors.

Discipleship Coordinator

First Impressions Coordinator

Choir Coordinator

Orchestra Coordinator

Widows and Orphans Coordinator

Health Coordinator

Transportation Coordinator

Community Projects Coordinator

Day Trips Coordinator

Missions Trips Coordinator

Tour Coordinator

On-Call Helper Coordinator

Bible/Book Study Coordinator

Exercise Class Coordinator

Prayer Coordinator

Hospitality Coordinator

30 Suggestions for Appreciating Senior Volunteers

Celebrating servant hearts & hands

At the organizational meeting described previously, the Planning Committee will establish some initial goals and scope of the Senior Adult Ministry for your church.

It is crucial to remember the words of Earl Nightingale here, "People with goals succeed because they know where they're going."

The committees mentioned on page 19 and the other ministry positions mentioned on page 22 will need leaders, or, directors. (The SAM Director cannot do it all effectively and efficiently!)

These leaders must constantly and continuously be told how much they are loved and appreciated for their ministry. Other seniors who are providing a service, in any of the ministries listed on pages 4 and 5, also need to be frequently informed of how much their ministry is also appreciated.

Listed below are just a few of the ways appreciation can be shown to these volunteers:

1. Show them the bigger picture.

No matter what they are doing, let your volunteers know the larger context – not just what they are doing, but why they are doing it – and you will show you respect them and appreciate their work.

2. Check in with your volunteers regularly…

… especially if they are in a remote location. If they are looking tired, give them a break. If they are looking bored, offer them a different task. (Are you familiar with the MBWA management concept?) *[Management by Wandering Around]*

3. Reaffirm their ministry.

Cast the vision for why they are critical to the ministry they are performing.

4. Send emails.

Every time a senior serves, send a "what to expect" email three or four days in advance; and a follow-up "thank you" email one day before serving.

5. Get to know them.

Nothing shows appreciation more than getting to know the personal lives of those who are volunteering.

6. Send a simple handwritten thank you card.

In the digital age that we live in, the handwritten card or letter is a novelty; and one that seniors will appreciate, as you convey your appreciation.

7. Ask for their thoughts and suggestions.

Before the ministry begins, ask for their thoughts. After the ministry is over, ask how it could be improved in the future.

8. Keep senior volunteers informed.

Don't impose a new policy or procedure without first talking it through with your volunteers. If possible, give them latitude to make adjustments.
9. Throw Celebration Parties regularly.

10. Create easy off-ramps.

Don't lock your seniors into a lifetime perpetual service. Mix it up!

11. Take pictures.

Share these pictures through emails, letters, or monthly/quarterly bulletins.

12. Use quotations from your seniors…

…in your spoken and written correspondence. They want to know they have been heard, and what they said was deemed valuable.

13. Calculate volunteer hours.

Calculate who and how long, and celebrate their milestones (# of days, hours, years, etc.)

14. Take more pictures.

15. Don't waste their time.

Make sure there is enough work for your senior volunteers when they arrive. Show appreciation by being prepared for their ministry.

16. Have the best equipment you can afford.

As much as possible, don't make people struggle to accomplish their task. Help them to make it easier.

17. Throw Celebration Parties regularly.

18. Send hand-signed birthday cards.

Seniors still appreciate this personal touch.

19. Food works!

The cost of not feeding volunteers is greater than what is spent on food.

20. Public appreciation.

Peer recognition goes far! Public appreciation translates into private loyalty. Identify a significant accomplishment, and have the rest of the team applaud them.

21. Thank you notes for families.

Thank their families for the part they play in allowing this senior to volunteer.

22. Remember milestones.

Create a system for remembering important dates.

23. Prepare them well.

Make their serving experience the best it can be. Anticipate any "bumps in the road". Anticipate any "surprises" that may arise. Brainstorm with your senior volunteers… they will appreciate that.

24. Be an encourager.

Everyone appreciates words of encouragement, written or spoken.

25. It's all about Jesus.

Every senior volunteer will appreciate seeing how their ministry connects to the gospel and changed lives; and, to the mission of your church and the building of God's Kingdom.

26. Respect their time.

We all have busy lives outside of our volunteering ministry responsibilities. So be prepared! Start on time. Return calls and emails promptly. By respecting their time, you value them as volunteers.

27. Throw Celebration Parties regularly, and take pictures!

28. Plan an Annual Senior Adult Ministry Volunteer Appreciation Dinner/Party.

29. Contact your local newspaper.

Send out press releases to your community newspaper(s), about the difference your seniors are making in the community. Encourage other community seniors to join the fun.

30. Ask for the Mayor's involvement.

Ask the city mayor, town council, and/or State/Commonwealth Representative to bestow some special proclamation for your volunteers after serving on a community project. Include pictures and names (newspapers like that.)

Should Jesus tarry... remember where you are heading:

Number of People Age 65 and Over and 85 and Over

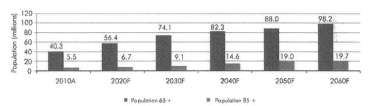

5 Keys to Effective Leadership

What does a leader do? The answers (and books) are endless. But there are five things every leader must do for the Senior Adult Ministry they lead.

1. Uphold Core Values

Every organization has a set of core values (at least, they should). It is the leader's job to uphold those values. To make sure they are followed, honored and embraced. If a core value is "excellence," then that value is only as real and formative as a leader makes it by upholding it throughout the organization.

Our Senior Adult Ministry Coordinators must have 10:

•   The Bible is true and the catalyst for life change.

•   Lost people matter to God, and, therefore, they should matter to us.

•   We aim to be culturally relevant while remaining doctrinally pure.

•   It is normal to manifest authenticity and to grow spiritually.

•   We want to be a unified community of servants stewarding our spiritual gifts.

•   Loving relationships should permeate the life of the church.

•   Life change happens best through relationships.

•   Excellence honors God and inspires people.

•   We are to be led by leaders and structured biblically.

- Full devotion to Christ is normal.

Our ministry is to uphold all 10; celebrating when one is fleshed out, and, admonishing when one is not.

2. Cast Missional Vision

If there was one task almost universally affirmed for a leader, it is casting vision. But not just any vision—it must be the casting of the missional vision of the local church. If we are "taking a hill", you need to define where the hill is, and why it is worth taking.

Meaning: "Here's the target on the wall. Here's what we're trying to do, and why."

On a more personal level, casting missional vision is helping individuals see how they are contributing to the vision of the church in ways that expand their own vision about their investment.

It's walking up to a person serving in a Senior Adult Ministry and saying: "I'm so glad you're serving. Thank you. Because of you, there's someone in the service able to explore what Christ can mean for their lives. That's what you're doing."

3. Create Unity

The Bible teaches that the number one requirement for becoming a leader is leading your own personal family well. Why? Because we are a family. Almost every organization would be best served by being led as if it were a family. The question is whether it is a functional family or a dysfunctional family. The answer lies in whether the "parent leader" does the hard work of keeping everyone unified relationally.

A good leader works to bring parties together, work through conflict and create open lines of communication.

That is the goal, organizationally.

4. Give Permission

Only a leader can give permission. This is not about control, but the privilege of turning people loose. A leader enables people to develop their gifts, chase ministry dreams, take risks and explore new ventures. In fact, the Apostle Paul wrote in the New Testament letter of Ephesians that the job of a church leader is to equip people for ministry. A leader clears the way for people to follow paths of God's design and leading.

Going further, a good leader sees things in people and encourages them to explore things they never dreamed of for themselves.

Therefore, it is not simply permission, but provocation. It is putting your arm around someone's shoulders and saying, "I see you doing this," or "I think you could make a difference here."

5. Develop Other Leaders

I don't know if I have ever read this statement (I can't believe it would be original to me), but I believe it to the core of my being: "Only a leader can develop another leader."

It's also one of the most important things we do.

So there are five things a leader must do. There are many more, of course, but these five?

All are musts.

14 Step Goal Setting Process for your Senior Adult Ministry

1. Decide exactly what you want in every key area of your ministry.

Start by idealizing. Imagine that there are no limitations on what your ministry can be, have or do. (God is able to do EXCEEDING abundantly.)

Three Goal Method – in less than 30 seconds, write down your three most important goals you have for your SAM ministry, right now. Write quickly.

Whatever your answer to this "Quick List Method" way of writing three goals it is probably an accurate picture of what you really would like to see.

2. Write it down.

Your goals must be in writing. They must be clear, specific, detailed and measurable. You must write out your goals as if you were placing an order for your goal to be manufactured in a factory at a great distance. Make your description clear and detailed in every sense.

3. Set a deadline.

Your subconscious mind uses deadlines as "forcing systems" to drive you, consciously and unconsciously toward achieving your goal on schedule. If your goal is big enough, set sub-deadlines.

If your goal is a God-sized goal, you may need to set a 1, 2, 5, 10-year goal, and then break it down, year by year.

If for some reason you don't achieve your goal by the deadline, simply set a new deadline. There are no unreasonable goals, only unreasonable deadlines.

4. Identify the obstacles that you may have to overcome to achieve your goal.

The Theory of Constraints: there is always one limiting factor or constraint that sets the speed at which you achieve your goal.

The 80/20 Rule applies to constraints. Fully 80% of the reasons that are holding you back from achieving your goal are inside yourself. They are the lack of a skill, a quality or a body of knowledge. Only 20% of the reasons you are not achieving your goal are on the outside. Always start with yourself.

5. Identify the knowledge, information and skills you will need to achieve your goal.

Especially, identify the skills that you will have to develop.

You can make more progress by going to work on the one skill that is holding you back more than any other.

Key Question: "What one skill, if you developed and did it in an excellent fashion, would have the greatest positive impact on your area of ministry?"

What one skill, if you developed and did it consistently, in an excellent fashion, would help you the most to achieve your most important goal for your ministry group? Whatever the skill write it down, make a plan and work on it every single day.

6. Identify the people whose help and cooperation you will require to achieve your goal.

Make a list of every person in your life, or group, that you will have to work with or work around to achieve your goal.

Start with the members of your family, whose cooperation and support you will require.

Especially, identify the people in your ministry area whose support you will need.

Once you have identified the key people whose help you will require, ask yourself this question, "What's in it for them?" Be a "go-giver" rather than a "go-getter."

To achieve big goals in your ministry, you will have to have the help and support of lots of people. One key person at a certain time and place in your life and ministry, will make all the difference. The most successful people are those who build and maintain the largest networks of other people whom they can help, and who can help them in return.

7. Make a list of everything you will have to do to achieve your ministry goal.

Combine the obstacles that you will have to overcome, the knowledge and skills you will have to develop, and the people whose cooperation you will require. List every single step that you can think of, that you will have to follow, to ultimately achieve your goal.

As you think of new items, add them to your list until your list is complete.

When you make out a list of all the things you will need to do to achieve your ministry goal, you begin to see that this goal is far more attainable than you thought.

You've heard before: "A journey of a thousand miles begins with a single step." You can build the biggest wall in the world one brick at a time; and, you can build the largest Senior Adult Ministry by reaching one goal at a time.

8. Organize your list into a plan. You organize this list by arranging the steps that you have identified by sequence and priority.

Sequence – what do you have to do before you do something else, and in what order?

Priority – what is most important and what is less important?

The 80/20 Rule says that 80% of your results will come from 20% of your activities. The 20/80 Rule says that the first 20% of time that you spend planning your goal and organizing your plan will be worth 80% of the time and effort required to achieve the goal.

Planning is very important; don't try to skip this step.

9. Make a plan. Organize your list into a series of steps from the beginning all the way through to the completion of your goal.

When you have a Goal and a Plan, you increase the likelihood of achieving your goals by 10 times, by 1000%!

■ Plan each day, week and month in advance.

■ Plan each month at the beginning of the prior month.

■ Plan each week the weekend before.

■ Plan each day the evening before.

The more careful and detailed you are when you plan your activities, the more you will accomplish in less time. The rule is that each minute spent in planning saves 10 minutes in execution. This means that you get a 1000% return on your investment of time in planning your days, weeks and months in advance. And your ministry will be much more effective, and you will reach many more seniors.

10. Select your number one, most important task for each day.

Set priorities on your list using the 80/20 Rule.

Ask yourself this question: "If I could only do one thing on this list, which one activity is most important?" Whatever you answer to that question, put a number "1" next to that activity.

Then, ask yourself, "If I could only do one other task on this list, which one task would be the most valuable use of my time?" Then write a number "2" next to that task.

Keep asking this question, "What is the most valuable use of my time on this list?" until you have your seven top tasks, organized by sequence and priority.

Here is another question you can ask, "If I could only do one thing all day long, which one activity would contribute the most value to my work and to my goals?"

Focus and Concentration are the keys to success. Focus means that you know exactly what it is that you want to accomplish, and concentration requires that you dedicate yourself to doing only those things that move you toward your goal.

11. Develop the habit of self-discipline.

Once you have decided on your most important task, resolve to concentrate single-mindedly on that one task until it is 100% complete.

Your ability to select your most important task and then to work on it single-mindedly, without diversion or distraction, will double and triple the quality and quantity of your output and your productivity.

Single Handling is one of the most powerful of all time management techniques. This means that when you start with the task, you avoid all distractions and stay with that task until it is done.

12. Practice visualization on your goals.

Create clear, vivid, exciting, emotional pictures of your goals as if they were already a reality.

See your goal as though it were already achieved. Imagine yourself enjoying the accomplishment of this goal.

In visualizing, take a few moments to create the emotions that would accompany the successful achievement of your goal. A mental picture combined with an emotion has an enormous impact on your subconscious and your superconscious mind.

Visualization is perhaps the most powerful faculty available to you to help you achieve your goals faster than you ever thought possible.

When you use a combination of clear goals, combined with visualization and emotionalization, you activate your superconscious mind. Your superconscious mind then solves every problem on the way to your goal. Your superconscious mind activates the Law of Attraction and begins attracting into your life people, circumstances, ideas and resources that will help you to achieve your ministry goals even faster.

13. Goal-Setting Exercise

Take a clean sheet of paper and write the word "Goals" at the top of the page along with today's date. Discipline yourself to write out at least 10 ministry goals that you would like to accomplish in the next year, or in the near future.

Begin each goal with the word "I." Only you can use the word "I." Follow the word "I" with an action verb that acts as a command from your conscious mind to your subconscious mind.

Finally, when you write down your goals, always write them in the positive, present tense. Instead of saying, "I will organize a community project," you would say, "I am a community project coordinator." Do you see the difference it makes?

Always state your goals as though they were already a reality, as though you had already accomplished them. This activates your subconscious and superconscious minds to change your external reality so it is consistent with your inner commands.

14. Decide upon your major definite ministry purpose.

Once you have written out a list of 10 goals, ask yourself this question, "If I could achieve any goal on this list within 24 hours, which one goal would have the greatest positive impact on my groups ministry?"

Whatever your answer to that question, put a circle around that goal. Then, transfer the goal to the top of a clean sheet of paper.

1. Write it down clearly and in detail.

2. Set a deadline on your goal and set sub-deadlines if necessary.

3. Identify the obstacles that you will have to overcome to achieve your goal, and identify the most important one, internal or external.

4. Identify the knowledge and skills you will need to achieve your goal, and the most important skill that you will have to become excellent in.

5. Identify the people whose help and cooperation you will require, and think about what you can do to deserve their help.

6. Make a list of everything you will have to do to achieve your goal. Add to the list as you think of new things to do.

7. Organize your list by sequence and priority, by what you have to do first, and by what is most important.

8. Make a plan by organizing your list into steps from the first to the last, and then resolve to take action on your plan, every single day.

9. Plan your goal in terms of the activities that you will have to engage in to achieve it, daily, weekly and monthly, in advance.

10. Set priorities on your list and identify the most important thing that you can do every single day to move most rapidly toward your ministry goal.

11. Discipline yourself to concentrate single-mindedly on the most important thing that you can do today until it is 100% complete. Practice single-handling with every major task.

Thanks to Brian Tracy for the above goal setting thoughts, provided to me via email.

Conclusion

Resolve in advance that no matter what happens, you will never give up. Persistence is self-discipline in action. Each time you persist and overcome the inevitable failures and disappointments you will experience, you become stronger and better. You develop stronger and deeper character. You increase your self-esteem and self-confidence, and your ministry advances the Kingdom of Heaven through your Senior Adult Ministry group.

Your ministry goal is to eventually become "Unstoppable", leading your ministry to greater heights every week, month, and year.

Decide exactly what you want, write it down, make a plan, and work on it every single day. If you do this over and over again until it becomes a habit, you will accomplish more in the next few weeks and months than most people accomplish in several years. Begin today!!!

May God richly bless you, your family, your Senior Adult Ministry, and your church!!!

Made in the USA
Coppell, TX
19 July 2023

19367229R00044